The Science of Waves and Surfboards

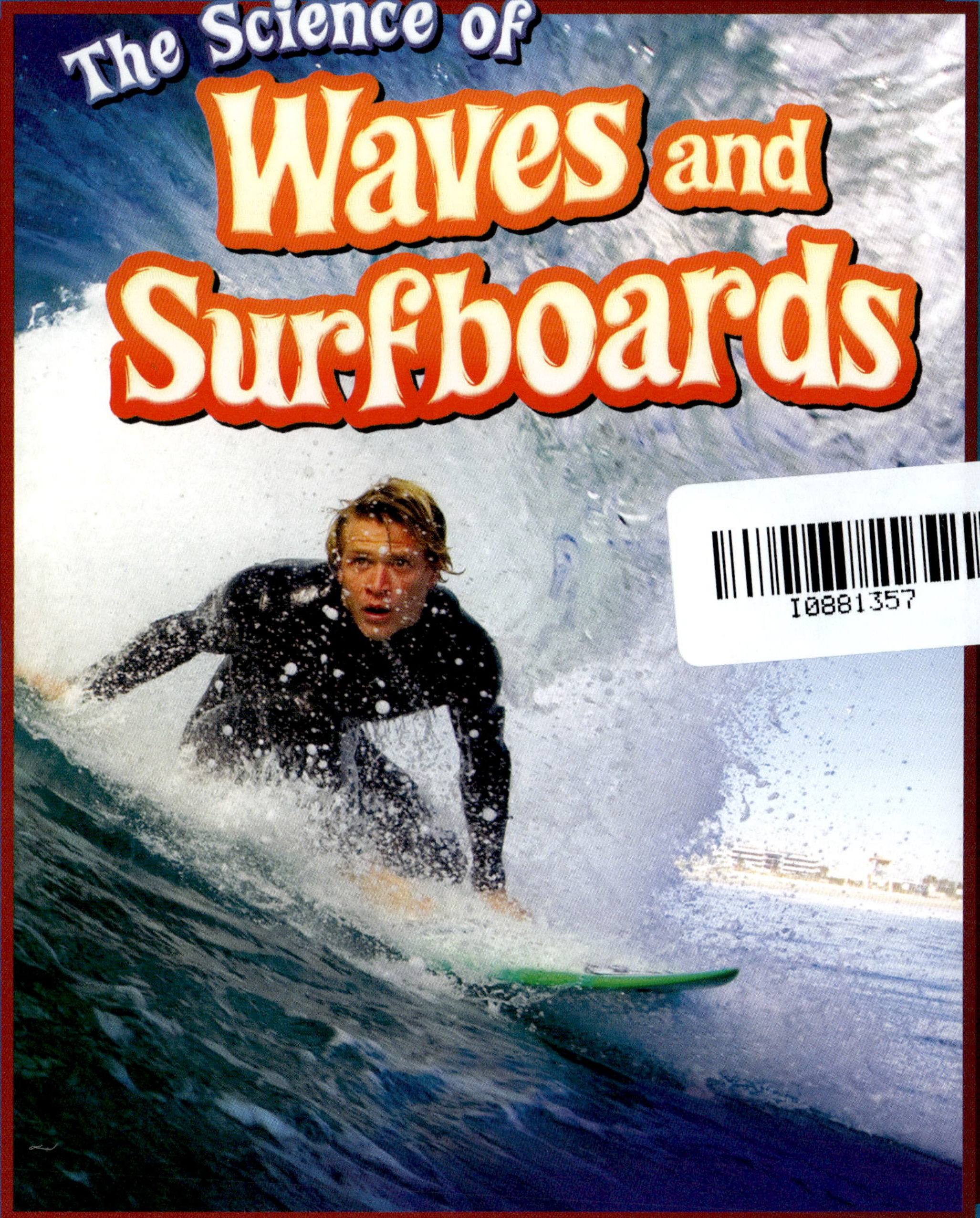

Lisa Steele MacDonald

Smithsonian

Contributing Author

Heather Schultz, M.A.

Consultants

Jeffrey Brodie
Supervisory Museum Program Specialist, Lemelson Center for the Study of Invention & Innovation
National Museum of American History

Tamieka Grizzle, Ed.D.
K–5 STEM Lab Instructor
Harmony Leland Elementary School

Stephanie Anastasopoulos, M.Ed.
TOSA, STREAM Integration
Solana Beach School District

Publishing Credits

Rachelle Cracchiolo, M.S.Ed., *Publisher*
Conni Medina, M.A.Ed., *Managing Editor*
Diana Kenney, M.A.Ed., NBCT, *Series Developer*
June Kikuchi, *Content Director*
Véronique Bos, *Creative Director*
Robin Erickson, *Art Director*
Seth Rogers, *Editor*
Mindy Duits, *Senior Graphic Designer*
Smithsonian Science Education Center

Image Credits: pp.2–3 lmspencer/Shutterstock; p.4 (left) © Smithsonian; p.5 (insert) Public Domain; p.6 (bottom), p.8 (bottom), p.14 Timothy J. Bradley; p.7 Digital Media Pro/Shutterstock; p.11 Courtesy Cancock/Stab Magazine; p.12 (left) Jorge A. Russell/Shutterstock; p.12 (right) Courtesy of Russell and Nina Love/calsurfpix; p.15 Kirk Wester/Shutterstock; p.18 EQRoy/Shutterstock; p.20 Everett Collection/Newscom; p.21 Public Domain via Wikimedia; p.22 North Wind Picture Archives/Alamy; p.23 (top) Guerilla / Alamy; p.24 (top) Allen J. Schaben/Los Angeles Times via Getty Images; p.24 (bottom) Joel Guy; all other images from iStock and/or Shutterstock.

Library of Congress Cataloging-in-Publication Data

Names: MacDonald, Lisa, author.
Title: The science of waves and surfboards / Lisa Steele MacDonald.
Description: Huntington Beach, CA : Teacher Created Materials, [2019] | Includes index. | Audience: Grade 4 to 6. |
Identifiers: LCCN 2018005463 (print) | LCCN 2018016083 (ebook) | ISBN 9781493869459 (E-book) | ISBN 9781493867059 (pbk.)
Subjects: LCSH: Surfing--Juvenile literature. | Surfboards--Juvenile literature. | Ocean waves--Juvenile literature. | Wave-motion, Theory of--Juvenile literature. | Sports sciences--Juvenile literature.
Classification: LCC GV839.55 (ebook) | LCC GV839.55 .M24 2019 (print) | DDC 797.3/2--dc23
LC record available at https://lccn.loc.gov/2018005463

Smithsonian

Teacher Created Materials
5301 Oceanus Drive
Huntington Beach, CA 92649-1030
www.tcmpub.com

ISBN 978-1-4938-6705-9

Printed by: 926. Printed in: Malaysia. PO#: PO16413

Table of Contents

Catching a Wave

From the shore or on television, surfing might seem like magic. Skilled surfers make it look like riding even the biggest waves takes no effort at all.

But surfing requires a lot of athleticism and knowledge. In fact, the sport relies on science. Without **buoyancy**, surfers would sink. Without acceleration, they would not be able to travel the length of a wave.

Science also plays a role in how surfboards are made. Early surfers used planks of wood as boards. They learned by trial and error which materials and shapes worked best. They could only use materials that were native to their homes. Today's surfboards are the results of years of research, engineering, and applied science.

The history of surfing is a lesson of the progress in science. So, dive in and find out more!

Duke Kahanamoku was a popular surfer from Hawai'i in the early 1900s.

1882 engraving of surfers in Polynesia

One of the first reports on surfing comes from Mark Twain. The author tried and failed at "surf-bathing" during a trip to Hawai'i in 1866.

The Science of Surfing

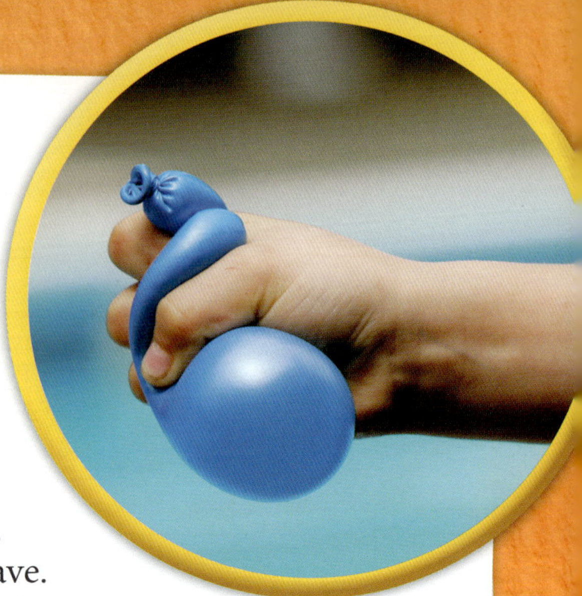

Imagine you are holding a water balloon. If you squeeze it, the balloon bulges out on one side or another. As your hand squeezes, the water pushes out on the balloon. This creates pressure in different places. In a similar way, opposing forces act on water in a wave. One force pushes down, and one pushes up. The energy creates pressure. This pressure is what pushes a surfer through a wave.

Three factors combine to create a successful ride. First, surfers need the motion provided by waves. Second, they need an item to give them buoyancy—a surfboard. Third, they need balance and control to help them stay in the right place on the board and feel comfortable moving the board in the water. These three things act together to create a thrilling ride.

The world record for longest time and distance surfed on open water is 3 hours and 55 minutes! Gary Saavedra surfed a man-made wave created by a boat.

The Motion of the Ocean

Water in the ocean is always moving. This movement can form waves and currents. Ocean waves are energy that travels on the surface of water toward shore. Ocean currents are moving water far beneath the surface of the water. Meanwhile, air is moving water above the surface of the water.

At first, wind travels across the water freely. The **ripples** pick up speed and get larger and more powerful. By the time the water nears land, it is moving quickly and with great force.

As a wave gets closer to shore, water becomes more shallow. The ocean's bottom current slows when it hits the sloping sea floor. The ocean's top current continues to move at the original speed. When the top moves faster than the bottom, a wave begins to form.

As the top current rushes on, the bottom moves up to meet it. This upward movement of water becomes the **face** of the wave. This is where surfers ride.

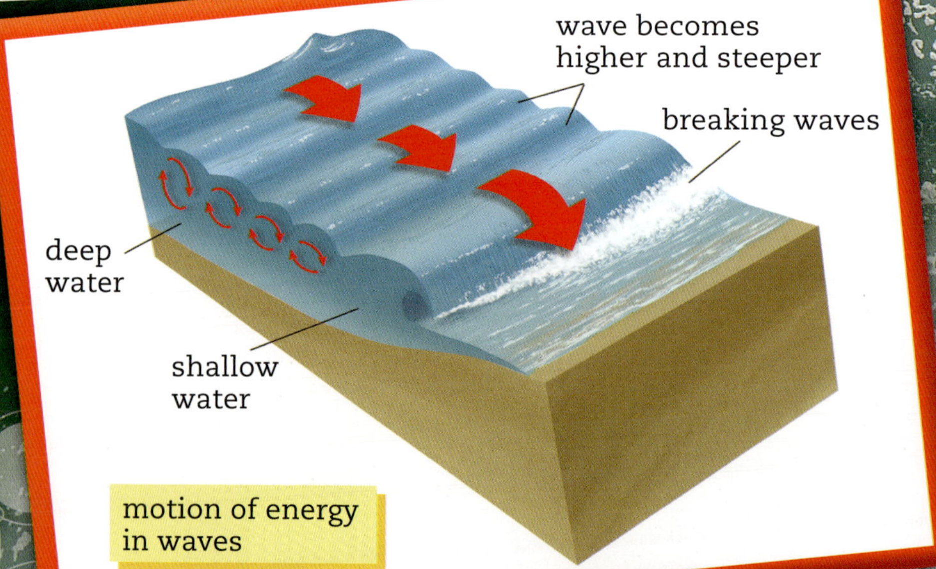

motion of energy in waves

Surfers spend most of their time paddling out and waiting for waves. For every hour they spend in the water, only about five minutes is spent actually riding waves.

When you see surfers waiting on their boards in a **lineup**, it is because they know where waves will form. The shape of the ocean floor does not change much from day to day. So waves form in the same places.

Ready to Ride

Surfers' rides begin when they paddle into forming waves. Surfers must adjust their speeds to match the speeds of the waves. The larger the waves, the faster surfers must paddle.

At the top of waves, gravity pulls on surfers and their surfboards. This pull helps surfers gain more speed as they ride down the faces of waves. The pull of gravity is strongest in the top one-third of waves. So surfers try to stay there as long as possible.

TECHNOLOGY

Dock Surfing

In 2017, surfers tried a new way to catch waves off the coast of Bali, Indonesia. They ran! A 30-meter (about 100-foot) floating dock was built where waves formed. Surfers paddled out to the dock and waited for waves. Then, they ran along the dock and jumped onto waves with their surfboards. This gave them the speed they needed without paddling into position.

In Control

When surfers get low on waves, they sometimes perform a move called a cutback. It is when surfers quickly turn their boards back up a wave. Then, they turn their boards back down when they are near the top of waves. They ride up the faces of waves and then use gravity to surf down waves. Surfers use the force and strength of this motion, or **momentum**, to ride for as long as they can.

By making small changes in their stances, surfers can **alter** how boards travel on waves. Most of the time, surfers keep their stronger foot close to the tail of a surfboard. This is because a surfer's back foot helps to control the turn of the board. Shifting body weight and pressing down on the back of the board will turn it and keep its nose out of the water.

A surfer does a cut back.

MATHEMATICS

Quite a Ride

Velocity, or speed in a certain direction, and gravity create **g-forces**. These are the same forces that push you back in your seat in a speeding car. Surfers feel strong g-forces when they turn at the bottom of a wave. One company built surfboards that measure the g-forces surfers feel. The measurements show that surfers feel more force than what is felt by a drag racer, an astronaut, or a roller-coaster rider!

Anatomy of a Surfboard

Choosing a board is not just about looks. There are a few things surfers must consider before choosing the board they want. First, they need to know the kinds of waves they will be surfing. If they surf small, slow waves, surfers should choose one kind of board. If they surf large, fast waves, they should choose a different board.

Next, surfers must decide the kind of ride they prefer. Do they want a board that offers a slow and steady ride? Or do they want a fast and furious ride? A beginner might need a board that helps them stay balanced. And an experienced surfer might be looking to learn some new tricks.

There are many kinds of surfboards—longboards, shortboards, guns, fish, **hybrid** boards, and others. There are advantages and disadvantages to each type of board. To choose, a surfer needs to understand how surfboards work.

Surfboards come in many shapes and sizes.

SCIENCE

Even Spread

When people stand on land, their body weight is concentrated in their feet. In water, that concentration is why people sink. A surfboard spreads weight evenly over a large area. The bigger and wider the board, the more a person's body weight is spread out.

How They're Made

Most surfboards today are made with a chemical foam core, which helps them float. There are different kinds of foam, and some are denser than others. The denser the foam, the stronger the surfboard. This makes it less likely to break while riding fast waves.

A surfboard's core needs support to make the finished board durable and strong in the water. For that, a strip of wood is added down the center of a board. It is called the stringer. With stringers, boards do not bend as much, making them less likely to break.

The foam core is wrapped in a cloth made of fiberglass and is then coated with resin. Fiberglass is very stiff when dry, which gives a board more support. Resin seals the board and gives it a smooth texture. Each layer added to a board makes it stronger, but it also affects a surfboard's weight.

Fiberglass is cut and put in place.

Resin is applied over fiberglass sheets.

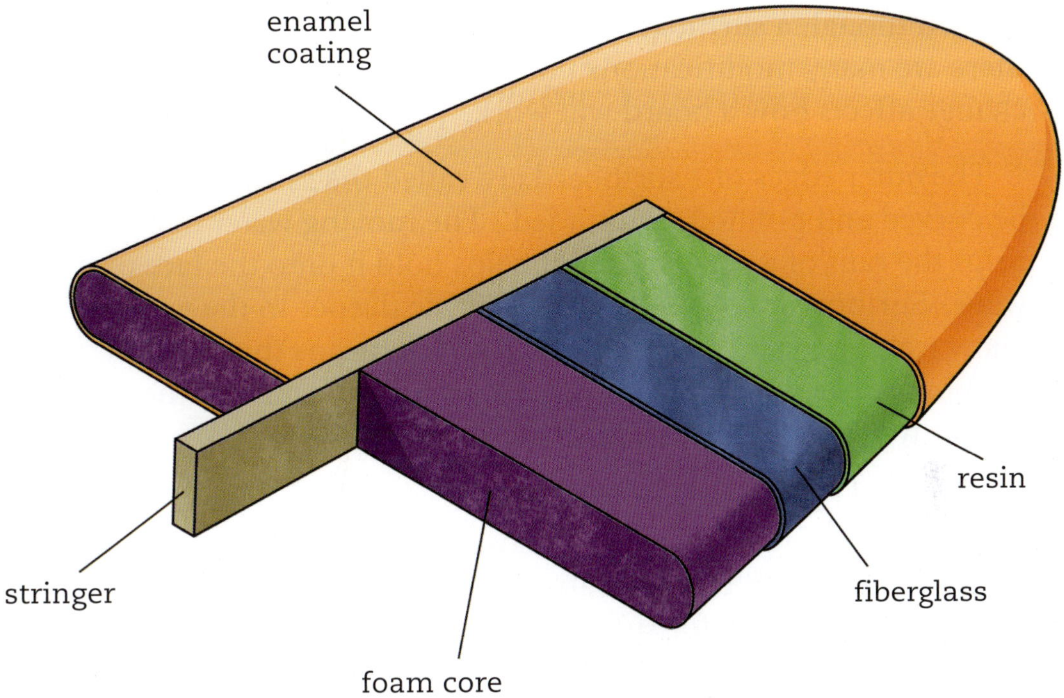

ARTS

Signature Shapes

If science tells people the best shape for a surfboard, why don't they all look the same? There are two main reasons. The first is that every wave is different, so the "right" shape depends on the wave. Second, for many years surfboards have been crafted by hand. Shapers spend years improving their skills and are proud of their craft. People can tell who makes each board by their distinct styles.

Shaped with Purpose

Even though a surfboard looks like one piece of equipment, there are many modifications that can be made to it. Even a small change affects how a board will work.

The outer edges of a surfboard are called the rails. They can be curved and pointed or rounded. The moving water of a wave grips the rails of a surfboard and helps hold it onto the face of the wave. Surfboards with rounded rails ride deeper in the water and allow water to grip the board longer. This means that a board will be more stable. Boards with pointed rails are faster, but they are harder to turn.

The front of a surfboard is called the nose. It can also be rounded or pointed. A rounded nose is better for beginners. It keeps the front of a board floating in smaller, slower waves. A pointed nose is good for surfers who need more control in large, fast waves.

These surfboard designers shape their boards to have rounded rails.

The first surfboards were 3.6 meters (12 feet) long and weighed about 73 kilograms (160 pounds). You had to be strong and athletic just to get out to a wave!

At the other end of the surfboard is the tail. Its shape can change how fast a board will move and how much control a surfer will have. A round tail keeps a board stable but slow. A square or angular tail makes a board faster and move more easily.

The bottom of a surfboard is important, too. Some boards are smooth on the bottom, but others have grooves in them. Grooves change the way water flows under a surfboard.

Fins are on the bottom of a surfboard near the tail. Beginners usually use a board with one large fin and two smaller side fins to help keep their boards steady. As a surfer's skills improve, he or she may switch to a board that has smaller fins. They help boards turn more easily.

Choosing the right surfboard is important. To pick the right board, surfers need to know their skill level and the types of waves they will be surfing.

A woman gets ready to surf in the 1920s.

single fin board

surfboard fins

George Freeth was a Hawaiian surfer who brought the sport to California. His board was $2\frac{1}{2}$ m (8 ft.) long and weighed over 90 kg (200 lbs.).

George Freeth

Surfing through the Years

People began to put the science of surfing to use hundreds of years ago. Early surfers from Tahiti brought the sport to Hawai'i. Surfing was a status symbol for chiefs and nobles.

The first surfers cut planks of wood from local trees and used them as surfboards. These early boards were very long and heavy.

In the 1920s and '30s, boards became lighter. Surfers cut holes in the boards and glued thin sheets of wood over them. They mixed light woods, such as balsa, with strong woods, such as redwood. During this time, surfers began changing the shapes of their boards. They **tapered** the tails to move better in the curls of waves.

After World War II, fiberglass and chemical foam were used to make surfboards. They made boards stronger and lighter. Surfers also began moving from longboards to boards that were shorter.

engraving of Hawaiians surfing in the 1870s

A surfer prepares to add a veneer to his hollow surfboard.

ENGINEERING

Make Do

In the 1920s, surfer Tom Blake wanted to make his surfboard lighter. So he took his solid wood board and drilled hundreds of holes in it. He covered the board with a thin sheet of **veneer**. The result was a much lighter surfboard. People laughed when he first showed up to a competition with his hollow surfboard. But then, they saw how well it worked. His design changed surfboards forever.

Surfers on the West Coast made even more advances in surfboard design. They shaped boards for specific types of waves. In the 1960s, the shortboard was invented. The average board length dropped to 1.8 m (6 ft.).

The popularity of surfing spread from beach to beach around the world. Australians loved the new, lighter boards. Over the next three decades, surfers there created even better boards.

Surfing gained popularity thanks to movies such as *Gidget*, *Beach Blanket Bingo*, and *The Endless Summer*. Surfboards were made faster. They cost less, so more people could try the sport.

Innovation keeps coming in the world of surfing. Today, there are boards with GPS, radios, and even motors. Boards are being designed using computers. Who knows how surfboards will evolve next!

Laird Hamilton rides one of his inventions—the hydrofoil board.

In 1971, Pat O'Neill invented the modern surf leash. Tired of chasing after his board, he tied a length of surgical tubing to his leg and attached it to the board with a suction cup.

Surf's Up!

All around the world, people catch waves in early mornings, on weekends, and on vacations. Some people compete, but all of them surf for the joy of it.

All surfers love waves and the ocean. On the water, they can see the great power and thrilling forces of nature at work.

Surfing is science in action! Science explains why a surfer can charge down the length of a wave or fly up its face.

Surfing is part sport, part art, and part science. So, grab your surfboard, get out on the water, and enjoy the best science lesson nature can teach you!

STEAM CHALLENGE

Define the Problem

You and your friends like to surf, but it is tough to get all your boards to the beach. You saw a foldable kayak and are wondering whether you can create a foldable surfboard that would be easier to transport and still hold up after use.

Constraints: Your surfboard should not bend or buckle when placed in the water.

Criteria: Your foldable surfboard must reduce its length or width by at least one half and should be buoyant in water.

1 Research and Brainstorm

How will folding a surfboard affect buoyancy? What folded shape will be easiest to transport? What materials will work best? Are any extra supports needed at your folds? Search the Internet for ideas that might inspire you.

2 Design and Build

First, make a paper model of your surfboard to decide how your board will fold. Then, sketch your design. List materials you are using in your model and materials that could be used in an actual foldable surfboard. Then, build your model.

3 Test and Improve

Create waves in a container of water to test how your surfboard holds up. How did your board perform? Can you decrease the size of the folded surfboard even more? Modify your design and try again.

4 Reflect and Share

How might a foldable surfboard compare to a regular surfboard? Consider the pros and cons of each. Which would you prefer?

Glossary

alter—to change partly

buoyancy—the ability of an object to float on air or water

denser—more tightly packed or heavier than other things of the same size

face—a front, upper, or outer surface

fiberglass—a light and strong material made from thin glass threads

g-forces—the force of Earth's gravity or acceleration on a body

hybrid—having or produced by two or more different components

innovation—a new idea, method, or device

lineup—area where surfers wait to catch a wave

momentum—force or strength gained from motion

resin—a sticky material produced by trees that can be used to cover and protect

ripples—very small waves on the surface of a liquid

tapered—shaped in a way that gradually becomes smaller toward one end

velocity—speed in a certain direction

veneer—a thin sheet of wood or another material attached to the surface of something

Index

CAREER ADVICE
from Smithsonian

Do you want to learn about surfing?
Here are some tips to get you started.

"Study mathematics and science so you understand how waves and speed work. In high school, take physics classes to learn about motion. Those skills will help you improve your surfing."—*Jeffrey Brodie, Museum Program Specialist*

"Surfers are not the only 'wave chasers' out on the ocean. There are scientists learning about waves that occur on the ocean floor. Some of these waves are the size of skyscrapers. Where they go and what they will tell us is still not known. Maybe you can be the scientist who figures this out!"—*Emily Frost, Ocean Portal Managing Editor*